CAPTIVATED!

"Come with me...my bride!"

Song of Solomon 4:8

TAMMY HENDRIX

WESTBOW
PRESS®
A DIVISION OF THOMAS NELSON
& ZONDERVAN

WestBow Press books may be ordered through booksellers or by contacting:

WestBow Press
A Division of Thomas Nelson & Zondervan
1663 Liberty Drive
Bloomington, IN 47403
www.westbowpress.com
844-714-3454

ISBN: 978-1-6642-4116-9 (sc)
ISBN: 978-1-6642-4115-2 (e)

Print information available on the last page.

WestBow Press rev. date: 04/14/2022

Set me as a seal upon your heart! Song of Sol. 8:6

DEDICATION

With joy, I dedicate this book to my weekly prayer partners Tamar, Peggy, Nina, Carol, Judy, Carmen, and Patti. Also, to my Faithful Friends Sunday School Class. Your prayers absolutely get the attention of Heaven!

This is a collection of prophetic poems from the Lord. Some may not understand this type of poetry, and may think I am being judgmental. No offense intended. The Holy Bible is filled with prophetic imagery.

ACKNOWLEDGMENTS

Thank you, Criselda Barker, for your encouragement
and beautiful artwork. colivabarker@gmail.com

The Warrior Bride
colivabarker@gmail.com 2 Samuel 22:35

WEDDING DAY

The Captivated Bride

I sleep, but my heart is awake; It is the voice of my beloved!
Song of Solomon 5:2

LOVESTRUCK!

I lay on my bed as the orchestra of Heaven plays, and the angels strum their golden harps. Suddenly, I am taken up in a vision of my Beloved.

You say, "Come closer. Come higher!" So, I ascend to gaze upon your loveliness—the beauty of your face.

You say, "Come near, My fair one. I have mysteries to unfold. Expectantly, I humble myself on bended knee, as I reflect upon your lovingkindness, ever transfixed on your glory and majesty.

The King is my Beloved! I am lovestruck beyond words, as His great splendor and countenance transform me. Yes, the King is my Beloved, none can compare!

Song of Solomon 5:2 I sleep, but my heart is awake; it is the voice of my beloved! He knocks saying, "Open for me…"

THE SECRET PLACE

May your day be blessed with blessings from above. May you feel the caress of the Savior's love. May His love abound, and His plans unfold, as you sit in His Presence for hours untold, in the Secret Place (Matt. 6:6), under the glory spout where God's unmerited favor and grace is poured out. Let His wings cover you as a mother hen (Ps. 27:5), who gathers her chicks for protection and care, and against present dangers ahead, beware! No matter what the future may hold, God's love is a constant we can behold.

Let the Lord who is gracious shine His light upon you like twinkling stars on a moonlit night, giving peace to your world, no matter your plight, showing you the glorious plan of the Father and Son (Jer. 29:11). And, may the Holy Spirit guide you, as the Three-in-One, as you wrap your plans and your dreams in the arms of the One, who shed His Blood selflessly on Calvary's Tree, to see mankind soar to new heights, and be free!

May your blessings outnumber the sadness around you as you meditate on God's goodness, and His Spirit surrounds you. Because, the Lord is sovereign and His Kingdom reigns! So put on your crown and wear it with pride; the Father is forever faithful, and always by your side.

Matthew 6:6 When you pray, go into your room, and when you have shut the door, pray to your Father who is in the secret place...

HEAVEN'S PORTALS

The portals of Heaven are open this morning. The Father is calling, so quit your sojourning! Sit long in His Presence—rest there awhile. He has secrets to reveal, and promises to fulfill. Sit long in His Presence for His glory resides with those who are searching, for there rich treasure abides.

Angels ascend and descend upon Jacob's ladder (Gen. 28:12); the portals are open and time doesn't matter. Sit long in His Presence, oh, Glory Divine! He longs for a people that find in Him treasure, and searches for gold in glorious measure. Sit awhile at His feet, and your requests He will meet—just give Him your time, your gifts and your love for His good pleasure.

The portals of Heaven are open this morning. The Father is calling, so quit your sojourning! Sit long in His Presence—rest there awhile. He has secrets to reveal, and promises to fulfill. Sit long in His Presence for His glory resides with those who are searching, for there rich treasure abides.

Genesis 28:12 Then he dreamed, and behold, a ladder was set up on the earth, and its top reached to heaven; and there the angels of God were ascending and descending...

FIND TIME FOR ME

"Find time for Me, and you will see My glory and power radiating from thee."

"Find time for Me, let earthly pleasures flee, and you will be astounded by My favor on thee!"

"Find time for Me, and My glory you will see. Yes, find time for Me, and with My promises you will agree!"

2 Peter 1:3-4 As His divine power has given to us all things that pertain to life and godliness, through the knowledge of Him who called us by glory and virtue, by which have been given to us exceedingly great and precious promises, that through these you may be partakers of the divine nature...

Note: Prophetic Word the Lord gave me, personally.

DANCE!

There is a spirit of dance in this place! I leap and twirl with joy, and bow before my King. In adoration, I dance and sing. The atmosphere is changed, when praises ring.

Standing tall on pointed toe, or kneeling low on bended knee, my love and praise I lavish on Thee. To no one else could I go, for You are the lover of my soul!

My mourning is over, and a new day dawns. Joyfully, I spin and twirl in Your Presence, unashamedly. Like David danced, I will dance, too! You have ravished my heart (Song of Sol. 4:9); my life is yours, for it was never mine. I died to self, long ago. Yeshua-Jesus, you have ravished my heart, and this dance is for You!

There is a spirit of dance in this place! I leap and twirl with joy and bow before my King. In adoration, I dance and sing. The atmosphere is changed when praises ring.

Song of Solomon 4:9 You have ravished my heart with one look of your eyes.

I WILL WORSHIP

I have decided to get up and worship today, because I can't handle my problems any other way.

Night after night, tossing and turning in fright, wondering if it will ever end—the torment, the fear, the whispers of Satan in my ear. Does God really hear when we pray? I guess so, I've made it through another day. Night after night, day after day, as our prayers go out, sometimes still in our heart arises doubt.

I have decided to get up and worship today, because I can't handle my problems any other way.

Everything that is within me will give You praise. Every breath I take will lift You high! I have decided to get up and worship today…and every day, because I can't handle my problems and fears any other way.

Psalm 47:6-7 Sing praises to God, sing praises! Sing praises to our King, sing praises! For God is the King of all the earth…

I'VE GOT A PROMISE!

I've got a promise, and I'm hanging on. I'm hanging on to His strong hand—not in desperation, but in victory! Yes, I've got a promise and I'm hanging on!

I hear Him say, "I'll give you the victory, just trust in Me. Time is Mine, and all My promises are true."

I've got a promise, and I'm hanging on. I'm hanging on to His strong hand—not in desperation, but in victory! Yes, I've got a promise, and I'm hanging on!

"Trust not in the world; turn your focus to Me. Have I not promised My goodness you will see (Ex. 33:19)? My grace is sufficient (2 Cor. 12:9); clasp your hand in Mine. Walk forward into your promised destiny, and be free!"

I've got a promise, and I'm hanging on. I'm hanging on to His strong hand—not in desperation, but in victory! Yes, I've got a promise, and I'm hanging on!

2 Corinthians 1:20 For all the promises of God in Christ are yes, and in Him, Amen, to the glory of God...

Promise-1.) an oral or written agreement to do or not do something, vow 2.) indication, as of a successful prospect or future, basis for EXPECTATION

THERE IS A SONG IN YOU!

"There is a song in you! Let it out, sing it out, shout it out for the world to hear. I've put a song in your heart to lift others, not keep to yourself."

"Be an instrument of healing. Be a conduit of My love. For long I have sought you from realms above."

"Shut out the voices, it's time to unwind. Shut out the voices, so you can hear Mine! Live in a place of habitation, not mere visitation—near Me, in unending anticipation."

"There is a song in you! Let it out, sing it out, shout it out for the world to hear. I've put a song in your heart to lift others, not keep to yourself." …"Sing!"

Isaiah 65:14 Behold, My servants will sing for joy of heart.

TAKE MY HAND

"Take My hand and don't let go," the Father says, "I told you so! There will be days when life overwhelms you, causing more pain than you've ever known, but hold tight, I won't let you go. You are loved, you are cherished! I have a plan (Jer. 29:11). I will open doors no man can shut. I am your all—I am the I AM (Ex. 3:4)."

"Hold on tight, I have a plan. As we walk hand in hand, My plans will be established, My plans will unfold. I am the I AM, there is none other. I have seen your desperation, tears, and your brokenness. Let Me embrace you with the Father's love, as My desires become your desires, and My plans become your plans. I am the I AM, so take My hand!" ..."Hold on tight!"

Psalm 48:10 According to Your name, O God, so is Your praise to the ends of the earth; Your right hand is full of righteousness.

THE PRAYER MEETING

We show up, and You show out! We come to You, without a doubt (2 Cor. 5:7). It's time to move mountains (Matt. 17:20), not just drink from the fountains (John 4:14). There is great delight in knowing that the prayers we are sowing like flowers will bloom as a beautiful bouquet, a tantalizing array, a fragrance most pleasing to the King!

We know You hear us when we pray (2 Chron. 7:14), because Your Word declares it so. We bend our knees and humble our hearts, to hear from Heaven the plans established long ago (Jer. 29:11). Plans to give us a future and a hope. Plans You set in order from the start.

We show up, and You show out! We come to You, without a doubt (2 Cor. 5:7). It's time to move mountains (Matt. 17:20), not just drink from the fountains (John 4:14). There is great delight in knowing that the prayers we are sowing like flowers will bloom as a beautiful bouquet, a tantalizing array, a fragrance most pleasing to the King!

2 Chronicles 7:14 If My people who are called by My name will humble themselves, and pray and seek My face, and turn from their wicked ways, then I will hear from heaven, and will forgive their sin and heal their land.

THE SPIRIT AND THE BRIDE

The Spirit and the Bride say, "Come!" The Spirit and the Bride say, "Come!" (Rev. 22:17) Come with a new perspective. Come with a new objective.

Listen to what the Spirit is saying to the churches (Rev. 3:22). "Come!" "Oh, come!"

The Spirit and the Bride say, "Come!" The Spirit and the Bride say, "Come!" (Rev. 22:17) Come with a new perspective. Come with a new objective.

"I'm singing over you (Zeph. 3:17), wooing you with My love! I'm rejoicing over you with gladness. The Lord your God in your midst, the mighty One will save."

The Spirit and the Bride say, "Come!" The Spirit and the Bride say, "Come!" (Rev. 22:17) Come with a new perspective. Come with a new objective.

"There's a prophetic declaration sent out to save the nations. Won't you declare it with Me, and make a proclamation? It's the time of Jubilee (Hebrew, Year of release)! Oh, wait and you will see (Hab. 2:3)!"

The Spirit and the Bride say, "Come!" The Spirit and the Bride say, "Come!" (Rev. 22:17) Come with a new perspective. Come with a new objective.

Job 22:28 You will declare a thing and it will be established for you.

Note: 12.31.17 The Lord spoke to my heart, "New perception."

new-never existing before
perception-1.) the act of perceiving 2.) insight

IN THE STILLNESS

In the stillness I can feel God and His gentle hand, as He strokes my face.

In the stillness I can hear God; His still, small voice whispering in my ear.

In the stillness I can see God, and I feel His Presence all around me, like the brush of angel wings!

In the stillness I can touch God. As I reach out, I am captured in His loving embrace. Because, in the stillness …HE IS THERE!

Psalm 4:4b Meditate within your heart on your bed, and be still. Selah

BE A VOICE!

Be a voice in the wilderness showing others the way (Matt. 3:1-2). Be a voice in the wilderness, don't delay!

Show others the path, and light the way. With the love of the Father, hasten the day!

Time is short, and eternity is at hand. Strive to reach others—stretch out your hand. Pull them back from the brink of destruction, where Hell's fires burn fiercely with brimstone and hail. Be a voice in the wilderness, and let love prevail.

Be a voice in the wilderness showing others the way (Matt. 3:1-2). Be a voice in the wilderness, don't delay!

Matthew 3:1-2 John the Baptist came preaching in the wilderness... and saying, "Repent for the Kingdom of heaven is at hand!"

NEW DAY

"It's a new day, and I've got a new way! I say, it's a new day, and I've got a new way! The old way is gone. I'm doing a new thing. Can you not perceive it (Is. 43:19)?"

"It's a new day, and I've got a new way! I say, it's a new day, and I've got a new way! Old doors are closed, for I propose to bring you into the NEW, sparkling, shining and true! There My glory is revealed and your destiny is sealed."

"It's a new day, and I've got a new way! I say, it's a new day, and I've got a new way! My invitation to you is to walk into the new. New doors are opening, with a new view. Old things have passed away (2 Cor. 5:17), and the new you will pursue."

"It's a new day, and I've got a new way! I say, it's a new day, and I've got a new way! It's a new day. Don't go the old way. Opportunities are ahead, so keep pushing through; I'll be with you always, because I love you! Don't look back, except to reflect. It's a new day, and I've got a new way! I say, it's a new day, and I've got a new way!"

"Your best days are before you, oh, how I adore you! Many miracles I have set before you, so keep walking in faith. Just know I am for you and with this in mind, I implore you set your face like flint (Is. 50:7), and look straight ahead."

It's a new day, and I've got a new way! I say, it's a new day, and I've got a new way! With joy in your step, and a song in your heart, your path is made straight (Is. 40:4), as you enter the gate."

"Possess the gates of your enemies (see Gen. 24:60), who lie in wait, to see if you'll stumble and fall on your face. If that happens, get up and continue your race (2 Tim. 4:7). My Grace is extended in this new day, so come walk beside Me, as I clear the way."

"It's a new day, and I've got a new way! I say, it's a new day, and I've got a new way! Victory is sure, so don't hesitate. Run your race with endurance (Heb. 12:1), as I open wide the gate."

"It's a new day, and I've got a new way! I say, it's a new day, and I've got a brand new way!"

Isaiah 62:10 Go through the gates...

Go-1.) leave behind, proceed, to move off, depart 2.) to begin to move off, as in a race, used as a command 3.) to move ahead, toward, enter, pass through

Gate-an opening providing passageway

Possess-to hold as property, occupy

Prophetic Word from God to me 12.15.17

I'VE CALLED YOU OUT!

"I've called you out, to call you in" I say, "I've called you out, to call you in. Spend time with Me on bended knee, and My glory displayed you will surely see! My glory will be revealed, oh you will see! Because, I've called you out, to call you in; yes, into My marvelous Kingdom of Light (1 Pet. 2:9). Rejoice, sons and daughters of the King; let My anthem ring, let it ring loud and ring far across this land. Just take My hand and take a stand. For victory you will see, because I've called you out to call you in."

"No time to hide. Spread My Kingdom message far and wide. It's time to shout the victory! Let My love be spread abroad, and you will see. Rejoice, rejoice, rejoice, servants of the King!"

"I've called you out, to call you in!" I say, "I've called you out, to call you in. Spend time with Me on bended knee, and My glory displayed you will surely see! My glory will be revealed, oh you will see!"

1 Peter 2:9 But you are a chosen generation, a royal priesthood, a holy nation. His own special people, that you may proclaim the praises of Him who called you out of darkness into His marvelous light.

SANCTUARY

"The preparation has been made; time spent in My Presence, and the foundation is laid. Joy and rejoicing are the keys to overcome and bring the victory."

"Those who worship Me in Spirit and in truth (John 4:24), will be greatly rewarded—for it is in praise and worship that the enemy's plans are thwarted!"

"Make My Presence your sanctuary, and your peace will be sweet. All it takes is to spend time sitting at My feet."

John 4:24 God is Spirit, and those who worship Him must worship Him in spirit and truth.

BE STILL

"Be still and know" (Ps. 46:10), that you can live in My overflow! Stay calm, I bring peace—just sit at My feet. Look high, look low, look everywhere you go; My miracles will surround you, just look around you!"

"Out of My abundance your needs are met. It's your John 10:10 moment, receive it as so! Life more abundant (John 10:10), and lavishly so, I present to you in My overflow! So, be still (Ps. 46:10), for I will come with a blessing, and a promise fulfilled. A promise to love you like no one has ever, a promise to give you My grace and new sight—to see things as I see, and depend solely on Me."

"For life is a vapor (Ps. 39:5, James 4:14) that vanishes quickly. Keep your eyes fixed on your Beloved (Song of Sol. 6:3), your King. Problems seem smaller in the Presence of the King, your guide, your protector, lover and friend. I am extravagantly, excessively, profusely pouring out of My overflow, great abundance into your life this day! Be still and know (Ps. 46:10). You will live in the overflow of life more abundant, for the Word established long ago, declares it so! Just, be still and know."

Psalm 46:10 Be still and know that I am God; I will be exalted above the nations, I will be exalted in the earth!

IT'S BEGINNING TO RAIN!

The rain is coming. Are you ready? The rain is coming, slow and steady—to wash us clean and send revival, no more mediocre, purposeless survival. Cast cares and umbrella to the wind. It's time for celebration, my friend!

With joy jump in, turn and spin! Times of refreshing come from the Presence of the Lord (Acts 3:19). Rejoice, jump in, and be restored!

The rain is coming. Are you ready? The rain is coming, slow and steady—to wash us clean and send revival, no more mediocre, purposeless survival. Cast cares and umbrella to the wind. It's time for celebration, my friend!

Acts 3:19 Repent and be converted, that your sins may be blotted out, so that times of refreshing may come from the presence of the Lord.

IF YOU COULD SEE!

"If you could see the end from the beginning…oh, if you could see! My plans are higher. You are living too low. Live higher, dream bigger than you ever have before!"

"If you could see the end from the beginning…oh, if you could see! Oh, if you could see, it would set you free! I've been preparing you for this day, for all eternity."

"Take My hand and run with Me into your future and destiny. Rejoice and sing! I'm redeeming the time (Eph. 5:16), just as I promised you. For the last will be first and the first will be last (see Matt. 20:16). Run with Me and sing Heaven's songs. I have much to show you. Stand firm. Be strong."

"If you could see the end from the beginning…oh, if you could see! Hold tight. Don't give up. Joy comes in the morning (Ps. 30:5), and this joy will surround all your days. So, grab the horns of the altar (Pray-see Ex. 27:1-8), and press through!"

"Rejoice, dance and sing, for I am coming to redeem. You've lost much in the battle, but you are highly esteemed by the Father, and the Son, the Holy Ones who have seen your tears and unending pain. If you could see the end from the beginning…oh, if you could see!"

Psalm 30:5 Weeping may endure for a night, but joy comes in the morning.

THE TIME IS COMING

The time is coming, and yet now is, when the eyes of the Lord will roam to and fro (2 Chron. 16:9), across the land, to see who is watching and waiting (Luke 12:37) for His return.

There is a call going out, can you hear it? A call to repentance. A call to holiness. And, a call to stand tall in full armor (Eph. 6:10), for the days ahead.

The sun is rising on a new day! It's time to get dressed in full battle array (see Eph. 6:10). Majestic white horses are getting ready to ride! They are stomping their feet in anticipation, muscular and strong.

Yahweh is coming! Yahweh is coming! Make yourselves ready—a people prepared and adorned with the beauty of His holiness. A Church shining with His glorious Light!

2 Chronicles 16:9 For the eyes of the Lord run to and fro throughout the whole earth, to show Himself strong on behalf of those whose heart is loyal to Him.

THE LION IS ROARING!

The Lion of Judah is His name. The Lion of Judah is His claim to fame. He's roaring, and He wants to roar through you!

He wants to roar through you...He wants to ROAR through you! There are nations in distress, how could we do any less?

The Lion of Judah is His name. The Lion of Judah is His claim to fame. He's roaring, and He wants to roar through you!

Be brave, be strong and sing the victor's song. He's roaring and He wants to ROAR through you. There's a wall of fire around you, so lift your banner high, and His voice do not deny.

The Lion of Judah is His name. The Lion of Judah is His claim to fame! He's roaring and He wants to roar through you!

There is a roar inside of you, and it wants to come out! What will you do? Will you stand as a valiant soldier true? On that great and terrible Day of the Lord, many will fall by the sword. He wants to roar through you. He wants to ROAR through you!

He is waging war with the hosts of Hell, but only the Lion of Judah will prevail. He wants to roar through you...He wants to ROAR through you!

Be brave, be strong, and sing the victor's song. He's roaring, and He wants to ROAR through you! There's a wall of fire around you, so lift your banner high, and His voice do not deny.

Revelation 5:5 But one of the elders said to me, "Do not weep. Behold, the Lion of the tribe of Judah, the Root of David, has prevailed...

VICTORY

Oh, great army of the Lord, it's time to draw your battle swords!

How can we win the victory, if our minds are not stayed on Thee (see Isa. 26:3)? Rejoice! Rejoice, and you will see! The Lord of Hosts, Jehovah-Sabaoth, will fight for you and bring you liberty.

Oh, great army of the Lord, it's time to draw your battle swords!

Worship Him with dance and song, for the battle won't be long. Shout His praises and decree (Job 22:28), and you will surely see! The Lord of Hosts, Jehovah-Sabaoth, is His name! March on soldiers of the Cross, victory is yours, you will not suffer loss. Brandish your sword at the enemy. Push back the darkness, and the devil will flee.

Oh, great army of the Lord, it's time to draw your battle swords!

2 Samuel 22:35 He teaches my hands to make war, so that my arms can bend a bow of bronze.

THE DARK NIGHT IS OVER!

I'm starting to sing again. I'm beginning to live! His love is unending—He gives and He gives.

The dark night is over, my joy has returned. With anticipation and expectation, my heart is renewed. My sadness has turned to gladness for my weary heart is joyful now, and forever will be!

I'm starting to sing again. I'm beginning to live! His love is unending—He gives and He gives.

Tomorrow looks brighter, my heart is lighter, and the full picture I see. Heaviness and sighing no more will be! I've been transformed through every storm, because my God is faithful, and I have His guarantee. For He changes not (Mal. 3:6), no matter my lot. Through valleys and trials I've walked many miles, but steadfast is He who walks beside me.

I'm starting to sing again. I'm beginning to live! His love is unending—He gives and He gives.

Psalm 100:2 Serve the Lord with gladness; Come before His presence with singing.

OH, I FEEL LIKE DANCING!

Oh, I feel like dancing! There is a spring in my step, joy in my heart, and a song on my lips.

It's time to go into the Chambers of the King, to dance and sing! Nothing held back, because He is worthy, so worthy, our Eternal King.

Oh, I feel like dancing! There is a spring in my step, joy in my heart, and a song on my lips.

The King is exalted, enthroned in the clouds. His glory shines brightly; His splendor displayed! His virtue flows freely, as I give Him praise.

Oh, I feel like dancing! There is a spring in my step, joy in my heart, and a song on my lips.

It's time to go into the Chambers of the King, to dance and sing! Nothing held back because He is worthy, so worthy, our Eternal King.

Psalm 33:1 Rejoice in the Lord, O you righteous! For praise from the upright is beautiful.

SHINE!

"It's time to shine, O Church of Mine! Arise and shine, because it's almost time for Jesus to split the eastern skies. He's looking for those that He can trust, and to illuminate His Presence is a must!"

"Don't hang your head in despair, when you see wickedness everywhere. Turn your face to the Son, the Holy One, God's only Begotten Son, who hears your sighs, and answers your cries. The Son of Man has a plan to defeat the enemy on every hand."

"It's time to shine, O Church of Mine! Arise and shine, because it's almost time for Jesus to split the eastern skies. He's looking for those that He can trust, and to illuminate His Presence is a must!"

"It's time to shine, O Church of Mine! Don't delay. Shine today, for there is no other way. Shine bright, shine strong, and show the world to whom you belong. With joy go out and bring them in, and let everyone see the Light within."

"It's time to shine, O Church of Mine! Arise and shine, because it's almost time for Jesus to split the eastern skies. He's looking for those that He can trust, and to illuminate His Presence is a must!"

"The One who was nailed to the Tree defeated all darkness and won the victory. Wave His banner high, and don't deny the Blood He shed in your stead. Your greatest days are just ahead!"

"It's time to shine, O Church of Mine! Arise and shine, because it's almost time for Jesus to split the eastern skies. He's looking for those that He can trust, and to illuminate His Presence is a must!"

"Live pure and undefiled, and in your mouth let there be no guile. For the days ahead may be full of dread, but the Church of Christ has Good News to spread. Stand strong. Stand tall. Share the message of heaven with one and all!"

"It's time to shine, O Church of Mine! Arise and shine, because it's almost time for Jesus to split the eastern skies. He's looking for those that He can trust, and to illuminate His Presence is a must!"

"Don't follow the crowd, or go the way of the lost. Time is short. Count the cost. Turn away from sin, boisterous talk and drink. Turn the world upside down (see Acts 17:6b), with your faith and actions! At all cost, point the lost to the Father, who resides in Heaven. It's almost midnight and the trumpet will sound joyfully for those prepared. But, it will be a sound of despair for those living in darkness, those who accepted Satan's whisper that they could wait. By believing the lie that there will be plenty of time, they have sealed their fate!"

"It's time to shine, O Church of Mine! Arise and shine, because it's almost time for Jesus to split the eastern skies. He's looking for those that He can trust, and to illuminate His Presence is a must!"

Mark 16:15-16 "Go into all the world and preach the gospel. He who believes and is baptized will be saved…"

IN REMEMBRANCE

"Take the Bread, take the Cup, and in remembrance lift them up. In remembrance for all I have done. In remembrance that the race has been won (see 2 Tim. 4:7)! All of Hell trembles, as all of Heaven rejoices. The victory is Mine, and I give it to you. Never doubt the depth of My great love and passion so true!"

"Lift the cup, My Blood shed for you. Lift the Bread, in remembrance of My body broken in two. My side was pierced, blood and water ran free—My heart held no grudge, only compassion for all to see."

"Take the Bread, take the Cup, and in remembrance lift them up. In remembrance for all I have done. In remembrance that the race has been won (see 2 Tim. 4:7)! All of Hell trembles, as all of Heaven rejoices. The victory is Mine, and I give it to you. Never doubt the depth of My great love and passion so true!"

John 6:48 I am the bread of life.

WAKE UP CALL

"Wake up, My complacent ones! Do you not hear My love song over you? Do you not hear it? Listen close. Tune your ears to the sound of My voice. I am your Beloved. I am! Hear the melody of songs from Heaven, as I rejoice over you with songs of love. Sing with Me, as I embrace you. Don't delay. The time is here. The time is now! Come close and let Me hold you. I want to whisper in your ear the delights of Heaven, the promises you have been waiting long to hear. I rejoice over you with singing, and I quiet you with My love (Zeph. 3:17). Come closer, even closer, than you ever have before!"

"Wake up, My complacent ones! Do you not hear My love song over you? Do you not hear it? Listen close. Lean into Me, as I reveal Myself to you. Wake up! Lean in. Listen close. I am your Beloved (Song of Sol. 4:2), and I am singing over you."

Zephaniah 3:17 The Lord your God in your midst, the Mighty One will save; He will rejoice over you will gladness, He will quiet you with His love, He will rejoice over you with singing.

HOPE

We have this hope in us (1 Peter 1:3). It's not time to give up. It's not time to give in. Show the world His brilliance...put it on display! Share the Messiah wherever you go, because time is short, and He loves us so.

We have this hope in earthen vessels (1 Peter 1:3). Be a vessel of honor and service to the King. His Kingdom reigns forever and ever, so His praises sing!

Magnify His Majesty and bid Him, "Enter in!" His Kingdom is within us, when we repent of sin. Let all the people and the nations of the Earth rejoice!

We have this hope lest we forget (1 Peter 1:3), so give Him honor; sing His praises! The excellence of the power is the treasure within (see 2 Cor. 13:5).

2 Corinthians 4:7 We have this treasure in earthen vessels that the excellence of the power may be of God and not of us.

HIS GLORY REVEALED

His glory is revealed in us sometimes through more than just His gentle touch. At times, it is revealed through the many trials and tribulations that we face, for His namesake (Psalm 30:5, 2 Cor. 13:5).

The winds of adversity may roar, but on eagles wings we can take flight and soar (Is. 40:31)! If we press into Him, He will hide us under the shadow of His wings (Isaiah 91:4). No weapon formed against us will prosper (Isaiah 54:17), or even sting!

His glory is revealed in us, sometimes through more than just His gentle touch. At times it is revealed through the many trials and tribulations that we face, for His namesake (Psalm 30:5, 2 Cor. 13:5).

As with a shield (Psalm 91:4), He is protecting us from the enemy who comes to steal, kill and destroy (John 10:10). Though our adversary comes to us as a roaring lion, the Lion of Judah will prevail (1 Peter 5:8)!

His glory is revealed in us, sometimes through more than just His gentle touch. At times, it is revealed through the many trials and tribulations that we face, for His namesake (Psalm 30:5, 2 Cor. 13:5).

Mighty warrior, pick up the Sword of the Spirit (His Word, Eph. 6:10), and brandish it at the enemy! In battle array (Armor, Eph. 6:10), run toward the enemy and slay! He is defeated as the Lord fights for you (1 Peter 4:12); His glory revealed for all to see.

Ephesians 6:10-11 Be strong in the Lord and in the power of His might. Put on the whole armor of God, that you may be able to stand against the wiles of the devil.

DANCING WITH THE ANGELS

As I spend time with the Father, captivated by His Presence, the glory falls in this room! Angels on ladders from Heaven, transcending and descending in spectacular splendor to the Father, in supernatural dimension and flair. Bringing Heaven to Earth in glorious fashion, removing all gloom and doom in the air.

A Divine exchange is made between darkness and light, leaving a heavenly deposit of peace and joy everywhere. Though the angels aren't seen in my minds-eye, they are revealed, bringing excitement where once was despair.

The angels are dancing, leaping, twirling and spinning in midair! Should I join them, I ponder, do I dare?

With restraint thrown to the wind, I jump from my chair, leaping, twirling and spinning in midair! Because, tomorrow is not promised, but today is here. Life should be a party, with our joy increasing, year after year!

Sit, if you must, deep in your chair, but Heaven is calling, and there's no time to spare! Rejoice for joy at the invitation at hand! Live life large, boldly, and as extravagantly as you can! Lavish your love on the Father above, as he bids you to join Him, as tenderly as a dove (Song of Sol. 4:1). Your Bridegroom is waiting hand extended to you; all of His passion and desire He pledges anew.

Say, "Yes," and take this dance. It's a match made in Heaven. Rejoice, as He calls you by name!

Oh, the angels are dancing, and fanning the flame! All of Heaven is calling your name, "Come dance, My Beloved, cast restraint to the wind. I'll take the lead, just come closer to Me. My love will heal you, and set you free! Come dance with the angels, right next to Me."

Your Beloved is calling, "Oh, won't you be free? Take one step closer, and then you will see. There's joy in My Presence, so come dance with Me!"

"All of Heaven rejoices as captives are set free! Step out. Come beside Me, My beauty to see. Life's cares are fleeting, as you spend time with Me. Come closer My Beloved, and with JOY you will see, My hand is extended, so come dance with Me!"

Song of Solomon 2:4-5 He brought me to the banqueting house, and his banner over me was love. Sustain me with cakes of raisins, refresh me with apples, for I am lovesick.

THERE'S SOMETHING ABOUT CHRISTMAS

There's something about Christmas that makes people kinder. There's something about Christmas that serves as a reminder... that God is love!

His ways are gentle. His joy abundant. His peace immeasurable, as we dwell in His Presence, with hearts overflowing. Surrounded by unseen realms of angels on high, we breathe in deeply His glory and majesty.

There's something about Christmas that makes people kinder. There's something about Christmas that serves as a reminder... that God is love!

There's something about Christmas, it's in the air! There's something about Christmas that beckons us to be like Him, full of perfect love, for all His Creation. His loving example is set before us, as He shines His countenance on all who join Him in sharing His attributes and heart.

There's something about Christmas that makes people kinder. There's something about Christmas that serves as a reminder... that God is love!

John 15:12 This is My commandment, that you love one another as I have loved you.

MOURNING TO DANCING

My mourning has turned to dancing, I twirl with delight! The dark night is over, and hope is in sight.

Leaping, spinning, and dancing with all my might, I give God praise for how He handled the fight. The battle was fierce, but the darkness He pierced. Now, there is joy in my worship, as I honor the King!

My mourning has turned to dancing, I twirl with delight! The dark night is over, and hope is in sight.

He is worthy, so worthy of all my worship and praise. He turned my mourning into dancing, and set my heart ablaze! I lift my hands in worship, and will give Him all the honor and glory, for the rest of my days.

My mourning has turned to dancing, I twirl with delight! The dark night is over, and hope is in sight.

Jeremiah 31:13 "For I will turn their mourning to joy, will comfort them, and make them rejoice rather than sorrow."

LIFE IS PRECIOUS

Life is precious…every moment, every hour, of every day. Life is precious, and we should treat it that way.

Tomorrow is not promised, and today's clock is ticking. So, be careful to dream big dreams, and fulfill them. Because, life is precious and we are not promised another sunset, but we do have today!

Life is precious…every moment, every hour of every day. Life is precious, and we should treat it that way.

Enjoy life! Live and love with an excellent spirit, for the sand in the hourglass is quickly disappearing. Life is precious. Live today out loud, bold and in color!

Life is precious…every moment, every hour of every day. Life is precious, and we should treat it that way.

James 4:14 …you do not know what will happen tomorrow. For what is your life? It is even a vapor that appears for a little while and then vanishes away.

KEEP WALKING!

I've walked through some things that you would never dream! I've walked through some things that only God's peace could bring me through.

He will stand by you, and walk you through. With His mighty arm, He will protect you from destruction. Yes, with His instruction, He will walk you through!

I've walked through some things that you would never dream! I've walked through some things that only God's peace could bring me through.

I've walked through perilous times and situations, with much travail. Yet, God has never left my side, or caused my plans to fail.

With outstretched hand, He pulled me up, even when it seemed that I had no hope. His promises are true, and available for you. He will pick us up, out of any miry muck, because He loves us so, and the good news is He will never, ever let go!

I've walked through some things that you would never dream! I've walked through some things that only God's peace could bring me through.

My advice to you is, "Keep walking through! Take the Savior's hand, because He has a plan. A plan to prosper you, and give you hope (Jer. 29:11). So, grab that rope, that lifeline from Him, and keep walking!"

I've walked through some things that you would never dream! I've walked through some things that only God's peace could bring me through.

Jeremiah 29:11 I know the plans I have for you, declares the Lord, plans to give you a hope and a future.

NO MORE DECEPTION!

No more deception! My eyes are wide open. No more lies from the enemy, his bluff has been called. The game is now over. The end is in sight. No more deception, my God has won the fight!

My mind, and my heart belong to the Lord, my Beloved, my Savior has brandished His sword! His weapons of warfare annihilate the enemy's plans. His double-edged sword is firm in His hand!

No more deception! My eyes are wide open. No more lies from the enemy, his bluff has been called. The game is now over. The end is in sight. No more deception, my God has won the fight!

The battle is raging, but victory is at hand. So, I stand on the promises our Lord gave to man.

No more deception! My eyes are wide open. No more lies from the enemy, his bluff has been called. The game is now over. The end is in sight. No more deception, my God has won the fight!

Exodus 14:14 The Lord will fight for you, and you will hold your peace.

PRODIGALS ARE COMING!

The prodigals are coming from the East, South, West and North. The prodigals are coming out in full force!

Yes, the prodigals are coming without a hitch, the prodigals are coming out in full pitch. No longer enslaved by the things of this world, desiring to come home to the Father (see Luke 15:11-31), with arms open wide, resisting the devil, and swallowing pride.

The prodigals are coming from the East, South, West and North. The prodigals are coming out in full force!

Embrace them with fervor and forgive them their sins, that the joys of Heaven they may enter in!

With forgiveness and mercy fall fast on their neck (Luke 15:11-31), and weep with compassion as the Father and the angels rejoice!

The prodigals are coming from the East, South, West and North. The prodigals are coming out in full force!

Run to the prodigal and fall at his feet, and as Jesus forgave your trespasses and sin, be thankful the prodigal is outcast no more. A great celebration is at hand, no more retreat!

The prodigals are coming from the East, South, West and North. The prodigals are coming out in full force!

Luke 15::20 …and while he was still a distance away, his father saw him coming. Filled with compassion, he ran to his son, embraced him and kissed him.

BURN BRIGHT!

Choose to rejoice (Acts 3:19), and become a voice in this end-time revival. Dare to pick up the mantle, from the saints of old! Become an Elijah. Become bold! Let history be written on the hearts of those who burn for Him, in total abandonment and joy within. No more church as usual. No more church in a box. There is no life in dead works; for faith untested is lost!

Become a blazing torch and run your race (2 Tim. 4:7), with victory over sin. Hell is defeated, and death would have no sting (1 Cor. 15:55), if the saints would just praise Him, rejoice and sing!

Hearts won't be changed by religion and stuff, only a spirit of love and the Savior's touch. Burn bright, burn strong, and to you the victory will belong! Glow, glow, glow! Let your lovelight show, for the Father is searching far and wide for those who adore Him and will swallow their pride. Be the one and stay true, because Jesus, your Bridegroom is counting on you.

Matthew 3:11 "I indeed baptize you with water unto repentance, but He who is coming after me is mightier than I, whose sandals I am not worthy to carry. He (Jesus) will baptize you with the Holy Spirit and fire."

FIRE!

"There's a fire in you. What will you do? There's a fire in you, let it shine through! There's a fire in you, making all things new. Let it shine through you...let it shine through you! The trophy is won, and the battle is over!'

"There's a fire in you. Let it shine through! Declare (Decree, Job 22:28) My best from a place of rest. Yes, rest in Me, and you will see the victory!"

"There's a fire in you. Let it shine through! My purpose and plans have been established in the land (Jer. 29:11). So, rest in Me and you will surely see the victory. Be free! Be free! Free your mind from every care, sit at My feet and enjoy My Presence there. I will wrap you in My arms of love, and send angels from above. Angels to wage war on your behalf, as you sit with Me in heavenly places (see Eph. 1:3), and rejoice in Me!"

"In the deep dark night of the soul, remain steadfast and true and I will work wonders for you! For eye has not seen, nor ear heard of the things which I have prepared for those who love Me" (1 Cor. 2:9).

"Rejoice and sing! Honor your King, for in Me you will find liberty. Rejoice and sing! Let My fire burn bright in you. For I am "making all things new" (Rev. 31:5). There's a fire in you. Let it shine through!"

Job 22:28 You will declare a thing and it will be established for you; so light will shine on all your ways.

IT'S JUST FINE!

Yeah, I'm fifty-nine, and it's just fine! I can go where I want to, do what I want to, say what I want to (sometimes), and be what I want to. Because, well, I'm fifty-nine, and it's just fine!

I can play, if I want to, pay what I have to (Senior discount—Yippee!), stay if I want to, stray if I want to. Because, well, I'm fifty-nine and it's just fine!

Yeah, I'm fifty-nine, and it's just fine! I'm in the prime of my life, having the time of my life. It's all about attitude, so I'll keep a heart full of gratitude. No matter what comes or goes, I've learned to adjust, and keep my trust in the Man with the plan (Jer. 29:11), the great "I Am" (Ex. 3:14), for the Lord understands. He sees the direction of my heart's affection, so with pure joy I rejoice! Because, well, I'm fifty-nine, and that's just fine!

I'll choose to dance, choose to love, choose to smile, all the while. Because, I'm in the prime of my life, having the time of my life! It's all about attitude, so I'll keep a heart full of gratitude. I'll choose to rejoice, because that's the best choice. Yeah, I'm fifty-nine, and that's just fine!

Proverbs 19:23 The fear (reverence) of the Lord leads to life, and he who has it will abide in satisfaction.

DRINK FROM MY SPIRIT

"Drink from My Spirit. Oh, come and dine! Drink from My Spirit, do not be filled with wine. For the pleasures of this life none can compare, to My Presence and power, as My Word declares."

"There is joy in My Presence, not sorrow and despair. Yet, the world offers wine and drink unlike what My Spirit prepares! My "new wine" (Matt. 9:17) is costly, it requires your spirit and life to be intertwined with Mine. We two become one, as the Bridegroom and the Bride, putting aside all earthly desires, pleasure and pride."

"My Spirit will fill you with new wine so pure, that the things of this world will no longer allure!"

"Drink from My Spirit. Oh, come and dine! Drink from My Spirit, do not be filled with wine. For the pleasures of this life none can compare, to My Presence and power, as My Word declares."

Ephesians 5:18 And do not be drunk with wine, in which is dissipation, but be filled with the Spirit.

GIVE ME PRAISE!

"Give Me praise! Give Me praise, and I will exalt your nation. Give Me praise! Satan has a plan to keep you in the valley of defeat, but I have a miraculous plan (Jer. 29:11)—just lay prostrate at My feet. Give Me praise! Give Me praise!"

"I'm troubling the waters (see John 5:4), it's time to get in. I'm exalted in your praises. Give Me praise! Give Me praise! I'll make your way straight, as you enter by the narrow gate (Matt. 7:13-14). Give Me praise! Give Me praise! I'm exalted in your praises. Give Me praise! Give Me praise! I've whispered My promises to you up until now, but soon I will shout them from the mountaintop…just give Me praise. Give Me praise!"

"It will turn out for you as an occasion for testimony (Mark 9:11). Give Me praise! Give Me praise! I'm unfolding an anointing in you that is beyond measure. Give Me praise! Give Me praise!"

"When I am lifted up (John 12:32), all nations of people will be drawn unto Me…just give Me praise. Give Me praise! I'll give you a Word in due season (Jer. 20:9), as you give Me praise…all the praise!"

"No longer will the enemy attack, but he will flee (James 4:7). Give Me praise! Give Me praise! My plan you will see, just give Me praise. Give Me praise! Only believe (Mark 11:24), and I will be exalted in thee. Give Me praise! Give Me praise! Soon many will see how I shine in thee, just give Me praise. Give Me praise!"

"The Deliverer has come to set you free. Give Me praise! Give Me praise! Keep a grateful heart, and give Me all the glory. Obedience is the start (1 Sam. 15:22), just give Me praise. Oh, give Me praise!"

Psalm 43:1 I will bless the Lord at all times…

MY FATHER LOVES ME

I know my Father loves me and He hears my every prayer. I know my Father loves me, even when life does not seem fair. I just have to trust that He knows my every care. For I know my Father loves me, and He is always there.

He is there to wipe away my tears, and calm my every fear. I know my Father loves me, and to no earthly father does He compare. I know my Father loves me, of this I am aware!

He has been with me through thick and thin, and loved me even in my sin. I know my Father loves me, of this I have no doubt! So, I will trust Him through it all, and commit my way to Him.

I know my Father loves me, whether I'm on the mountain high or walking through the valley low. This I am sure of, because He has told me so. I am sure my Father loves me, and to Him my burdens go!

2 Corinthians 13:14 The grace of the Lord Jesus Christ, and the love of God, and the communion of the Holy Spirit be with you.

COME, OH COME!

Come, oh come, you weary ones! Come, oh come, hear Heaven's drums, beating with love from glory divine, calling out, "Oh wounded one, won't you be Mine? Now is the time. Don't delay! I'm only a prayer and a heartbeat away."

Come, oh come, you weary ones! Come to the Father and the Son, let the dance begin as you receive their love within, to reveal and heal the shattered and broken places.

Come, oh come, you weary ones! Oh, trust the One who gave His Son! Come, oh come, rejected ones. He loves you so, and He won't let go. Come, oh come!

Today is the day to cast care away. Walk forward in triumph! Don't look back; look straight ahead. It is for you Jesus' Blood was shed. Come, oh come!

John 17:12 While I was with them in the world, I kept them in Your name. Those whom You gave Me I have kept; and none of them is lost…

LISTEN NOW!

"Listen now, I've heard your cries! Listen now, daughter, I too have heard Satan's lies. Listen now, I am the I Am! Stand strong in Me, and I'll bring the victory!"

"Listen now! Listen now! This is the year of Jubilee, a time to be set free. It is an appointed time, a time set apart for laughter, and dancing. Wait and see! A time when dreams come true, for My faithful ones. A time of deliverance, and joyful singing."

"Listen now, daughter! Listen now! Listen for the sound of My voice. I am releasing freedom, supernatural peace, and My Spirit into your situation. Just listen, look and see!."

Jubilee-(Hebrew) "Year of release," Leviticus 25:8-13

Isaiah 26:3 You keep him in perfect peace whose mind is stayed on You, because he trusts in You.

TURN THE TIDE!

There's a deeper place in Him…go there! Go deep! Get lost in Him. Go deep; go wide! Be bold! Turn the tide! Turn the tide!

Be the one that He can trust. Change the world with His touch. Be bold. Turn the tide. Go deep, go wide! Get lost in Him, and show His love for all to see His Presence and power displayed in thee.

Be bold. Turn the tide. Go deep, go wide! The world is waiting and watching for those that will turn the world upside down (see Acts 17:6). Be that one, be bold!

Release the captives, set them free! Christ is counting on us, to bring liberty. There is freedom in Christ, and we have the victory! Be bold. Be strong. Turn the tide!

Proverbs 28:1 The righteous are bold as a lion.

HUSH

There's a holy hush in the atmosphere. It is holy, so holy. It is the excellent and majestic, magnificent Presence of the King!

Holy, holy is our God! Who can compare? Lofty, glorious and sublime—our King reigns!

Exalted in magnificence, grandeur and supreme authority, there is no one like Him. None have captivated hearts as our Sovereign Lord and King!

High and lifted up, the angels give Him the highest praise! Declaring His superiority over all, as they bow in reverence.

There's a holy hush in the atmosphere. It is holy, so holy. It is the excellence and majestic, magnificent Presence of the King!

Habakkuk 3:3 His glory covered the heavens, and the earth was full of His praise. His brightness was like the light; He had rays flashing from His hand, and there His power was hidden.

JOY JOURNEY

Let there be joy in my journey, this I request. Please, honor me Jesus, by giving your best. Oh, to sit in your presence morning, noon and night, raptured in the glory, as angels take flight!

Don't give me religion or the doctrines of men (Col. 2:22). There is no joy in that, in fact it is sin. Please, I urgently ask, let there be joy in my journey! Don't let religious spirits or doctrines of demons (1 Tim. 4:1), cart me out on a gurney!

Open my eyes to see spiritually that it's all about You, and none about me. You are the King highly favored, and truly adored! We all love You sincerely, but at times are wrapped up in cords...strong cords of deception, not setting us free. But, your Word says, "Who the Son has set free is free indeed" (John 8:36).

I will choose joy for my journey, and I'll hold your hand, as we run in this freedom to the heavenly land! Gone are the tears I've shed many years, for You are my hope and delight, as victory is sure and in sight.

I will not settle for religion or a church without vision (see Hab. 2:3). Time is short, and there are souls in the balance! It is time to awaken, Church, and find joy in the journey! Time is of the essence, and we will give an account to the Just Judge (Ps. 94:2) of our destiny and future. Run hard after God, because He is running hard after you! For our days are surely numbered (Ps. 90:12), and long we have slumbered.

Awaken the troops, grab your sword (Eph. 6:10), and march to victory! For His Word is truly a promise to you. Fight Hell's forces with a vengeance for soon you'll see, that God has given you much territory. The fullness of joy in your journey is the key. Joy will sustain you, through good times and bad, so march on, rejoice and be glad!

The floodgates of Heaven are about to burst forth! Take joy, be of good courage, and continually praise Him. Give Him honor, and with glee, send Satan's army on the run. For there is joy in the journey, if we have eyes to see!

My Savior is calling, He's beckoning me, to dance the dance of the victor, because I have been set free!

Habakkuk 3:18 Yet I will rejoice in the Lord, I will joy in the God of my salvation.

SEASON OF REST

There is a season of rest for the weary. Yes, a season of refreshing is upon us!

Lay down your cares, concerns and disappointments. He holds the key to set you free!

There is a season of rest for the weary. Yes, a season of refreshing is upon us!

Choose to rest in His Presence, and listen for His voice. His answer will banish all of your fears. And, with surety, He will answer all of your prayers.

There is a season of rest for the weary. Yes, a season of refreshing is upon us!

Stay close to the Father; let Him continually guide you. For His ways are much higher, and His love is much deeper than all the world has to offer.

There is a season of rest for the weary. Yes, a season of refreshing is upon us!

So, rest in His Presence; fling anxieties aside! Stay long under His sheltering wings of protection, and there abide (Psalm 91:4).

Acts 3:19 Repent therefore and be converted, that your sins may be blotted out, so that times of refreshing may come from the presence of the Lord.

RISE UP AND PLAY!

"Rise up and play!" we heard them say. "The Lord won't return for many a day. We will have our fill of love and wine, and then tomorrow we will rise up and dine (...the people sat down to eat and drink and rose up to play." Ex. 32:6). For He will not return today, let us go out and go our way. With joy we will sing and dance, so rise up and play, while we have the chance!"

"Rise up and play!" we heard them say. "You see, while the cat's away the mice will play. What's the rush? Why all the fuss? Rise up and play, the Lord has been gone for many a day. We still have lots of time to play. Hurray! Hurray! Rise up and play, for the Lord will not return, today."

"Then, to our dismay, the Lord did say," 'Your days are numbered (Dan 5:26-27, Ps. 89:12), for My House you have plundered (Is. 32:9-11), and in your complacency you have slumbered (Matt. 25:5 "But, while the bridegroom was delayed they all slumbered and slept."). Wake up, wake up, I say! You've had your time to dance and play. The hour is late, and time is short. Rise up, rise up and hear My voice!'

Exodus 32:19 So it was, as soon as he came near the camp, that he saw the calf and the dancing. So Moses' anger became hot, and he cast the tablets out of his hands and broke them at the foot of the mountain.

HIS PRESENCE

Spend time in God's Presence, those who know (Hebrew, "yada" intimately) His name. Spend time in His Presence, without refrain. Resist Him not…don't be like the children of Lot (Gen. 19:14)! Draw near to Him, while He may be found (Is. 55:6). He knows you by name, and He formed your frame (Ps. 139:15). Never disdain His love for you (John 3:16). He loves you with an everlasting love, and on your behalf He will send angels (Ps. 91:11-12) from above.

Spend time in God's Presence, those who know His name. Spend time in His Presence without refrain. Resist Him not… don't be like the children of Lot! Draw near to Him, while He may be found. There is a war going on in the heavenlies (see Eph. 6:12), but because of your prayers, He will send you warfare strategies (2 Cor. 10:4). Do not deny His love for you; stand as a soldier tried and true.

Spend time in God's Presence, those who know His name. Spend time in His Presence without refrain. Resist Him not…don't be like the children of Lot! Draw near to Him while He may be found. He's calling you out to call you in. The battle belongs to the Lord (2 Cor. 20:15), and in the end we WIN!

Spend time in God's Presence, those who know His name. Spend time in His Presence without refrain. Resist Him not… don't be like the children of Lot! Draw near to Him, while He may be found. There is joy unspeakable and full of glory (1 Peter 1:8), in the presence of the King. Yield your vessels and let His anthem ring! Through you, His power will be displayed (Dan. 2:22), so take up your sword (Word of God, Eph. 6:10), and walk in victory this day.

Seek His face, and He will show you His hand (strength and protection, Ps. 16:8). Seek His face, and He will give you the land (Josh. 13)!

Spend time in His Presence, those who know His name. It is time to put the enemy to shame (see 1 Col. 2:14)! It's in His Presence that we gather oil (Matt. 25:4), and in His Presence we gather the spoils of war. Do not delay, sit at His feet today. The hour is late, and some have already sealed their fate (Heb. 9:27)! Call out for mercy, from the Throne of Grace.

Oh, spend time in His Presence, those who know His name! Be like the wise maidens (Matt. 25:4), who refused to play. They didn't slumber (verse 13), when they were warned of the approaching Day (see Matt. 24:36). Our Bridegroom is coming and He will sweep away (Song of Sol. 3:6) those who have chosen to sit with Him daily, and embrace His ways. Refuse not His love, for He is calling you, today. 'Rise up, My fair one, I'll show you the way!'

Spend time in His Presence, those who know His name. It's a plea from the Father, so don't delay! 'How beautiful you are, my beloved…how beautiful (Song of Sol. 1:15). Rise up my beloved, my fair one, and come away (Song of Sol. 2:10)! Spend time in My Presence—don't delay!'

Matthew 25:6 And at midnight a cry was heard: 'Behold the bridegroom is coming; go out to meet him!'

THE WEDDING FEAST

There will be a day of reckoning, in the not too distant future. We will give an account to the Lord of Heaven, as we've laid men with men, not calling it "sin," and laid with women because it's our choice. We have given a voice to tolerance, being called judgmental, if we disagree.

The God of love, who lives above, looks down upon this tapestry we call our world with a sigh and a tear in His eye, and wonders why we've trampled on His holiness and purity. Then, on Judgment Day, as we've gone our own way, we'll give our reasons why wrong is right, and right is wrong (Rev. 14:12, Rom. 1:24-28). We'll try to defend our sin saying, "I didn't want to offend! I had no voice. I had no choice. Sin is sin…my desires crept in. Who are you to judge? God will understand."

But, sad to say on Judgment Day (Rev. 20:12-15), the Lord, the Righteous Judge (Rom. 1:18) will open the Book (of Life), and take a look, to see if our names are written in His Son's Blood, and forever sealed in the heavens above. Did we show love? Was our heart pure? Did our actions show we lived for God, or did we defile our holy temples, that were reserved for the Son (2 Cor. 13:5), who is the One who will call us to account? Are we pure and undefiled, or did our lusts run wild?

Our Lord said, "I am coming for a Bride (Believers) without spot or wrinkle (Eph. 5:27), who shines with My Light, and knows no night."

Darkness can't hide the deeds of men, when the Lord descends (1 Thess. 4:16). What will we say then? It will be too late, for we've sealed our fate (Matt. 25:12)! As we mourn our loss, counting the cost of our sin that brought an end to the choices we made, and the life we gave to this thing called sin.

As others, "Enter in..." (to the joy of the Lord, in Heaven, Matt. 25:21), we will watch in dread, as the One who died to redeem mankind, delivers our fate.

We will be sent away from the presence of the Holy One, the only begotten Son (John 1:14), the Lamb (Rev. 12:11) who knew no sin, but took our sin upon His back (Cross), so we would never suffer lack! He suffered and died for mankind, and at the end of time, is coming back for His Bride...Believers who have made themselves ready.

Arrayed in white at the Wedding Feast, His shinning ones He will call His friends (John 15:15), and with joy and rejoicing they will enter in!

So, keep watch (Matt. 25:13), and put away all sin, as it destroys and yokes to the very end. The Wedding Feast is close at hand! Until that day, let us go our way to love and pray, that all may join us with the Lord, and not fall by the sword.

The sword of wickedness is upon this world, but God in His grace is warning us to take our place. Shine bright, shine strong, because it won't be long before the Book is opened and our deeds laid bare. What will we say, in our despair...we didn't care or we weren't aware that Jesus died for all men everywhere? No time to run and have our fun, the wedding music is about to start, and Jesus, our Beloved (Is. 5:1), will judge our heart.

Matthew 22:2-3 "The kingdom of heaven is like a certain king who arranged a marriage for his son, and sent out his servants to call those who were invited to the wedding..."

NEW BEGINNINGS

"It's a day of new beginnings. Out with the old. In with the new. I say again, it's a day of new beginnings, so rejoice, rejoice, again I say rejoice! Dream bigger, dream wilder, dream bolder than you ever have before!"

"Don't stay in the valley, come up higher (Luke 14:10). I have much to show you, in this hour. In this new season, don't try to reason. It is a season of miracles and dreams come true. My great promises are coming to you!"

"It's a day of new beginnings. Out with the old. In with the new. I say again, it's a day of new beginnings, so rejoice, rejoice, again I say rejoice! Dream bigger, dream wilder, dream bolder than you ever have before!"

Isaiah 43:19 Behold I will do a new thing, now it shall spring forth. Shall you not know it? I will even make a road in the wilderness and rivers in the desert.

ABOUT THE AUTHOR

Tammy Hendrix has served in various levels of leadership within Aglow International over approximately thirty years, in local., state and regional positions including prison ministry. Her desire is to serve the Lord in whatever capacity He calls her into, but has a strong desire for prayer ministry, and a heart of love for the people and the land of Israel. She has been on four trips to Israel from 2000-2018, as well as a Mission Trip to the Dominican Republic. For the past twenty three years Tammy has been involved in a weekly prayer group in Alabama where she and her husband, Darrell, reside. In 2014 the author wrote a devotional book called, "I Choose To Rejoice!" Her most recent project is "Captivated!" which is a collection of prophetic poems and illustrations. And, she was honored to have prophetic Words of the Lord published on The Elijah List. A passion she has is to read of the moves of God from past church history, believing that a great end time revival is on the horizon. The best is yet to come!

Printed in the United States
by Baker & Taylor Publisher Services